WE
THE PEOPLE
DOLLEY MADISON

Library of Congress Cataloging-in-Publication Data

Klingel, Cynthia Fitterer.
   Dolley Madison.

   (We the people)
   Summary: A biography of the First Lady who, among her
other achievements, managed to save many state papers and a
portrait of George Washington from the invading British
who burned the White House in 1814.
   1. Madison, Dolley, 1768-1849—Juvenile literature.
2. Madison, James, 1751-1836—Juvenile literature.
3. Presidents—United States—Wives—Biography—
Juvenile literature.   [1. Madison, Dolley, 1768-1849.
2. First ladies]   I. Title.   II. Series: We the people
(Mankato, Minn.)
E342.1.K57   1987   973.5′1′0924   [B]   [92]   87-27148
ISBN 0-88682-167-3

WE
THE PEOPLE
DOLLEY MADISON

BELOVED FIRST LADY
(1768-1849)

CINDY KLINGEL

Illustrated By Nancy Inderieden

CREATIVE EDUCATION

DOLLEY MADISON

Little Dolley Payne was a merry child. But she wore gray dresses and plain bonnets. She was not allowed to dance or sing. A simple way of life was part of her Quaker faith.

Unlike most people who lived in America in the 1770's, the Quaker people believed in sending girls to school, instead of allowing only the boys to have that privilege. So Dolley had an education, unlike the daughters of the rich Virginia planters who lived nearby. She was smart and enjoyed school. She grew up to be clever and witty. She was very beautiful, too, even though her Quaker parents tried not to notice it.

After several years, life in Virginia began to change. In 1783, Dolley's father freed his slaves and moved to Philadelphia. Dolley didn't want to leave her friends behind. But she quickly made new friends, both men and women, in Philadelphia. When Dolley was twenty-two years old, she wed a young Quaker lawyer named John Todd. They were very happy together.

For many years, Americans had been fighting against the British in an attempt to gain independence. It was a hard fight, but finally America had won the Revolutionary War.

Philadelphia was now the capital of the United States. It was the most lively city in the whole country. Dolley's husband prospered.

They moved into a nice home. The marriage was a happy one, and two sons were born to the Todds.

Then, in August 1793, a terrible epidemic of yellow fever broke out in Philadelphia. Everywhere, people became sick.

John Todd rushed Dolley and their two sons out of the city so that they would not catch the disease. After he had them safely settled, he returned to help care for the sick. It was his duty as a Quaker. By doing this good work, he took sick himself. Longing to be with Dolley, he rode to the place she was staying and died in her arms.

Poor Dolley became very ill herself. Her baby, William, died. After some weeks, Dolley recovered.

During this time, the fever had disappeared in Philadelphia. People streamed back into town. Many of these people were officials of the government. Dolley, too, returned to Philadelphia. She was alone this time except for her little son, Payne. She was ready to face life without her husband.

In the spring, Dolley liked to go for walks with Payne. Her beauty caused men to stare in admiration. Among them was a 43-year-old "confirmed bachelor" named James Madison. He was a small man, only five feet, six inches in height. But his wisdom was gigantic. He was widely respected and was very active in government. He had helped develop the Constitution of the United States of America.

One day this important man asked to be introduced to the Widow Todd. Dolley was very nervous. She wrote to a friend, "Thee must come to me! The great little Madison has asked to see me this evening!"

They did meet that evening. They enjoyed each other's company, and Madison seemed to have fallen in love with Dolley almost at first sight. Not long after that evening, Madison asked Dolley to be his wife. Dolley was confused and wasn't sure what she should do. James Madison was not a Quaker. If she married him, she would be expelled from the church and from the way of life she knew so well.

Then Martha Washington, wife of President George Washington, sent for Dolley. Dolley was curious. She did not know why Mrs. Washington wanted to see her. When Dolley finally arrived, Mrs. Washington asked, "Is it true that you are engaged to James Madison?"

Dolley stammered, "No, I think not."

Martha said kindly, "If it is so, be proud of it. He will make thee a good husband, even though he is not of your Quaker faith."

Martha also told the amazed Dolley that even President Washington hoped she would marry James Madison. Mr. Madison had an important government career ahead of him. He had been alone for a long time. He needed someone special. A wife such as Dolley, full of charm

and wit could be a great help. And besides, he was in love with her!

Dolley was so surprised by what Mrs. Washington had said. Dolley wasn't sure just what to think! It made her feel good to know the Washingtons were in favor of the marriage.

After much thinking, Dolley agreed to marry James Madison. Although she greatly admired Madison, she still had some doubts in the back of her mind. She tried to ignore them, and she married James Madison on September 15, 1794. Before long, her admiration for him turned to sincere love.

They lived first in Philadelphia and then in Virginia. In Virginia, the Madison estate, Montpelier, had many visitors. Thomas Jefferson was the Madisons' neighbor. Montpelier became a popular meeting place where important men in government often came to confer. Dolley enjoyed having visitors, and her natural charm and friendly personality transformed her from a quiet Quaker housewife into an expert hostess. She put away her plain clothing and wore the latest styles. Her graciousness made even quarreling politicians friendly and smiling. Everyone enjoyed their visits to Montpelier. James Madison was very proud of his lovely new wife.

There were soon to be big changes in Dolley's new life, however. In 1801, Thomas Jefferson was elected President of the United States. He asked Madison to be his Secretary of State. This was an important job for Madison. Both he and Dolley were excited about what lay ahead.

The Madisons packed up and moved to the brand-new capital city, Washington, D.C. It was still mostly open fields and swamps. The "President's Palace," where Jefferson lived, was a gray, half-empty place. The Madisons were invited to live there. Jefferson was a widower, so Dolley became his hostess. Dolley was thankful for the many, many visitors she had entertained at Montpelier, for now she knew exactly how to entertain the most important people in America.

After living with President Jefferson for some time, James and

Dolley Madison moved into their own house. But Dolley continued her duties as unofficial First Lady. She also gave dances and parties at her own home that were the talk of Washington.

Jefferson was grateful for Dolley's glitter. It helped people forget the troubles of the infant United States. It began to look as though America and England would go to war again.

Jefferson served two terms as President of the United States. Then it was time to elect a new president. Who would it be?

It was James Madison! He was elected President of the United States in 1808, the fourth man to hold the highest office in the country.

Madison and Dolley once again moved into the President's Palace. This time, however, it was empty, as all the furniture had belonged to Jefferson. At Dolley's request, Congress set aside money to buy beautiful new furnishings that would remain in the President's Palace permanently. Dolley herself supervised the decorating.

As First Lady, Dolley brought an elegance to the United States capital. Her flair for entertaining became well-known. Foreign visitors, who had once scoffed at the "primitive" social life in Washington, now sat down to splendid meals or attended stately balls that were the equal of those in Europe. But Dolley did not forget the other people of Washington, those who were not important in government or foreign affairs. She also gave smaller parties and receptions for the common people. She even introduced egg-rolling on the presidential lawn on Easter Monday.

James and Dolley Madison enjoyed their four years at the Presidential Palace. The people liked Madison as their president and elected him to serve another four years.

In 1812, England provoked the United States to war. For the first two years of Madison's second term, the war went badly for the Americans. In 1814, the British invaded Washington itself.

Madison was away with the army. With the British on their way,

Dolley knew she would have to flee. Although frightened, Dolley stopped to think. She must save what she could from the Presidential Palace. She had servants pack up important papers from the office of the President. She even took down a large portrait of George Washington from the dining room wall.

When she had everything together, she drove away with her treasures. Luckily, Dolley had thought quickly, because not long afterward, the British set the city on fire. The President's Palace was destroyed. Dolley was considered a hero for her clever thinking.

In 1815, the war with the British ended. Washington was rebuilt. James and Dolley returned to Washington. They lived in a new home while they waited for the President's Palace to be rebuilt. Construction went slowly, however. Dolley continued her busy life of entertaining, but she missed living in the beautiful Palace.

Finally, the Palace, with its stone front newly painted white, was rebuilt and called the White House. The Madisons did not live in it again, however. The President's term ended in 1817, nine months before the rebuilding was completed.

The Madisons left Washington and returned to the peace of Montpelier, where they lived for the next twenty years.

James Madison died in 1836. Although Dolley had always loved

life at Montpelier, now it seemed too quiet. She decided to return to Washington, where she would find many friends and activities to fill her days.

In Washington, she became a social leader once more. People remembered her. Presidents Jackson, Van Buren, Tyler, and Polk were her close friends. She once again enjoyed the social life of the city. She felt at home among her friends and the people who loved her. She remained in Washington for many years until her death.

When Dolley Madison died July 12, 1849, the United States mourned its loss. She will always be remembered as one of Washington's most beloved First Ladies.

WE THE PEOPLE SERIES

WOMEN OF AMERICA

CLARA BARTON
JANE ADDAMS
ELIZABETH BLACKWELL
HARRIET TUBMAN
SUSAN B. ANTHONY
DOLLEY MADISON

INDIANS OF AMERICA

GERONIMO
CRAZY HORSE
CHIEF JOSEPH
PONTIAC
SQUANTO
OSCEOLA

FRONTIERSMEN OF AMERICA

DANIEL BOONE
BUFFALO BILL
JIM BRIDGER
FRANCIS MARION
DAVY CROCKETT
KIT CARSON

WAR HEROES OF AMERICA

JOHN PAUL JONES
PAUL REVERE
ROBERT E. LEE
ULYSSES S. GRANT
SAM HOUSTON
LAFAYETTE

EXPLORERS OF AMERICA

COLUMBUS
LEIF ERICSON
DeSOTO
LEWIS AND CLARK
CHAMPLAIN
CORONADO